Who Is
Hillary Clinton?

Who Is
Hillary Clinton?

by Heather Alexander

illustrated by Dede Putra

Penguin Workshop

To Merry—HA

PENGUIN WORKSHOP
An Imprint of Penguin Random House LLC, New York

Text copyright © 2016, 2019 by Heather Alexander, LLC. Illustrations copyright © 2016 by Penguin Random House LLC. All rights reserved. Published by Penguin Workshop, an imprint of Penguin Random House LLC, New York. PENGUIN and PENGUIN WORKSHOP are trademarks of Penguin Books Ltd. WHO HQ & Design is a registered trademark of Penguin Random House LLC. Printed in the USA.

Visit us online at www.penguinrandomhouse.com.

Library of Congress Control Number: 2016011728

ISBN 9780448490151 (paperback)   10 9 8 7 6
ISBN 9780399542343 (library binding)   10 9 8 7 6 5 4 3 2

Contents

Who Is Hillary Clinton?

When Hillary Rodham was thirteen years old, she wanted to become an astronaut. It was 1961. In one of his speeches, President John F. Kennedy promised that American astronauts would land on the moon by the end of the 1960s. Hillary dreamed of flying into outer space.

The idea was exciting and challenging, and that made Hillary want to do it even more. Hillary was not afraid of doing things few people had tried. So she wrote a letter to NASA (National Aeronautics and Space Administration). NASA is in charge of the United States' space program. She asked what she needed to do to become an astronaut.

Several weeks later, a letter came. It read: "We're not interested in women astronauts."

How could this be? Hillary was as smart, if not smarter, than any boy at school. She played softball with the boys. Why did being a girl matter?

"It was the first time I had hit an obstacle I couldn't overcome with hard work and determination, and I was outraged," said Hillary.

But when Hillary was growing up in the 1950s and 1960s, women faced many obstacles. They didn't have nearly the number of career choices that women do today. Back then, if a woman worked outside the home, she was usually a secretary, nurse, or teacher. Back then, women couldn't even buy a house or open a bank account in their own name. Society treated women as weaker and less intelligent than men.

Hillary promised that she would never let being a girl stop her from anything. And she didn't.

On June 6, 2016, she made history. She became the first woman chosen by a major political party to run for president of the United States. Although Hillary Clinton never became an astronaut, she has spent her whole life reaching for the stars.

CHAPTER 1
Standing Up for Herself

Hillary Diane Rodham was born on October 26, 1947, in Chicago, Illinois. Her dad, Hugh, owned a small business that made curtains. Her mother, Dorothy, stayed at home, taking care of Hillary and her two younger brothers, Hugh Jr. and Tony. Dorothy Rodham was a strong, loving woman, but she felt there had been many limits on what she could do with her life. She wanted more for her daughter.

When Hillary was three years old, her family moved to a brick house with a big backyard in the Chicago suburb of Park Ridge. There were forty-seven kids in her neighborhood! Front doors were left open, and kids ran in and out of everyone's houses. People often called Hillary a

tomboy. She loved playing softball and basketball, going swimming, and ice-skating on a nearby pond with her friends.

One day the kids on the block wouldn't let her play with them. Hillary ran home in tears. But her mother wouldn't let her in. "You have to stand up for yourself," her mother told her. She sent Hillary back outside. Hillary was scared. But she did stand up for herself—and it worked! After that, she was included in every game.

Hillary's father pushed her to do her best. "Can you do better than that?" he'd say. Hillary didn't mind. Unlike other fathers of girls, he never treated Hillary differently from her brothers. He taught her to throw a football, switch-hit in baseball, and take an interest in world events.

The Rodhams' dinner conversations often turned to politics. "I learned that a person was not necessarily bad just because you did not agree with him, and that if you believed in something, you had better be prepared to defend it," Hillary once wrote.

When Hillary was nine years old, some kids at school started saying she was "stuck up." But that wasn't true. Hillary had a secret. She often couldn't see if somebody was talking to her because she had bad eyesight and didn't like wearing her glasses.

But she needed her glasses, especially since Hillary loved to read. Every week she walked to the library with her mother. Her mother thought education was very important, especially for girls.

Hillary also loved being a Girl Scout, because she liked helping people. Near Hillary's home, there were big farms. Migrant workers from Mexico came to pick the crops. Migrant workers move from state to state when different crops are ready to harvest. They work long hours for little money.

Hillary wanted to help them. She babysat for their children. But she wanted to do more. So she and friends held a carnival to raise money for the migrant workers. This was the beginning of Hillary's life as an activist—someone who sees a problem and works to solve it.

Dorothy Howell Rodham

Born in 1919 in Chicago, Hillary's mom was one of nine children in her family. Her parents often left the kids by themselves. When Dorothy was eight, she and her three-year-old sister were sent on the train by themselves to live with their grandparents outside Los Angeles, California.

Dorothy's grandmother was a stern woman who wore long black dresses. When she discovered Dorothy had gone trick-or-treating on Halloween, she punished her. Dorothy couldn't leave her bedroom for a year, except to go to school. She couldn't even eat at the kitchen table!

Dorothy left her grandparents at age fourteen and found a job as a live-in babysitter. She was very poor. She had only one outfit that she washed by hand every night. After high school, Dorothy returned to Chicago and found a job in an office. There she met and married Hugh Rodham. But she always dreamed of college. While raising Hillary and her brothers, Dorothy read all the time. Finally, when she was in her sixties, Dorothy was able to take college courses. She died in 2011.

CHAPTER 2
A Time of Change

Hillary's family belonged to a Methodist church near their home. Hillary tried hard to follow Methodist teachings, particularly to, "do all the good you can, by all the means you can, in all the ways you can, as long as you ever can."

When Hillary was fourteen years old, Reverend Donald Jones joined her church. He was in charge of her youth group. In their neighborhood, everyone was white and well off. Reverend Jones wanted the youth group to understand what life was like for kids from other backgrounds. He brought the youth group to meet African American and Latino children from different neighborhoods in Chicago. From them, Hillary first learned about the civil rights movement,

Martin Luther King Jr., and Rosa Parks. Reverend Jones took the youth group to hear Dr. Martin Luther King Jr. speak in Chicago.

After the speech, Hillary got to shake Dr. King's hand! That's when Hillary decided that she, too, would fight for social justice.

In high school, Hillary was elected to the student council and served as vice president of the junior class. In her senior year, she ran for class president against several boys. But she didn't win. She wasn't upset, until one of the boys said, "You are really stupid if you think a girl could be elected president."

This made Hillary angry. Someday, she would show him!

After high school, Hillary went to Wellesley College in Massachusetts. Hillary liked that Wellesley was an all-women's college. Why? Because all the student leaders were women.

Many Wellesley students were caught up in the women's movement and feminism. Feminism says women and men should be treated equally. For instance, the same jobs must be open to them at the same pay. The women's movement was trying to pass laws to bring about equality. It made women's rights a political cause, one that Hillary deeply believed in.

Another political issue of the time was the war in Vietnam, a country in Southeast Asia. The United States was sending soldiers to fight in the war.

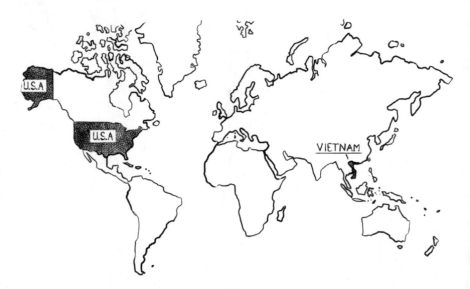

In America, many people—especially the young—didn't think the United States had any business taking part in this war. Hillary became one of them.

Hillary's concern about civil rights also grew in college. After Dr. Martin Luther King Jr. was shot and killed in Memphis, Tennessee, on April 4, 1968, she joined students in protest marches in Boston. She spoke out for the equality of all people, no matter their race or gender.

The Right to Vote

Since the early 1800s, all white men have had the right to vote in the United States. African American men got the right in 1870. But it wasn't until 1920 that women were finally allowed to vote.

Susan B. Anthony (1820–1906) and Elizabeth Cady Stanton (1815–1902) were two of the women who helped bring about voting rights.

Susan B. Anthony

Elizabeth Cady
Stanton

In 1872, Susan B. Anthony and fifteen other women were the first women to vote in a US election—and they were all arrested. Although neither Susan nor Elizabeth lived long enough to see their hard work pay off, the Nineteenth Amendment to the Constitution was finally passed in 1920, giving women the right to vote. In 1971, the voting age for everyone was lowered from twenty-one to eighteen.

The students at Wellesley admired Hillary and elected her president of the student government. When it was time to graduate, the students demanded that— for the first time—someone their age speak at the ceremony. Hillary was their choice.

Hillary stayed up the night before graduation, writing and rewriting. She was very nervous. She was still fixing her speech when she was called up to speak before all the graduates and their families.

Hillary said that she and the other Wellesley students had dreams that seemed out of reach. But they would no longer quietly accept the way things were for women. She encouraged the students to fight for a more fair world: "The challenge now is to practice politics as the art of making what appears to be impossible, possible."

Did people like her speech? Yes! The crowd gave her a standing ovation—for seven minutes! *Life* magazine even ran a story about her. At age twenty-one, Hillary was already in the public eye.

CHAPTER 3
Meeting Bill

Hillary planned to go to law school after college. She couldn't decide, however, if she should go to Harvard Law School or Yale Law School. She went to visit both. At Harvard, a friend introduced her to a famous law professor. The professor sniffed and said, "We don't need any more women."

Hillary chose Yale.

Yale Law School

She was one of twenty-seven women in a class of 235. A law school classmate said, "Hillary was one of those students you would know, because she would speak up in class when she had a point to make."

Hillary was noticed by another law student, too. His name was Bill Clinton. Bill liked how smart Hillary was, but he was afraid to talk to her. One day, they were both studying in the library. Bill was watching her from across the room.

Finally, Hillary couldn't take it anymore. She walked over to him. "If you're going to keep looking at me, and I'm going to keep looking back, we might as well be introduced. I'm Hillary Rodham."

Bill didn't know what to say. He suddenly couldn't remember his own name!

After that, they didn't speak for an entire year. But when they met again, they had *a lot* to talk about. They both were very interested in politics. Soon, Bill became Hillary's boyfriend.

One day, a former Yale Law School graduate spoke to the students. Her name was Marian Wright Edelman. Edelman knew that children could not do well at school if they were hungry, cold, tired, or not cared for properly. So Edelman started the Children's Defense Fund (CDF) to end child poverty in America. Hillary wanted to help. She remembered how her mother had grown up.

Marian Wright Edelman

"Her sad and lonely childhood was imprinted on my heart," said Hillary. Edelman gave Hillary a summer job. Hillary learned a lot about health and education. The work made her want to focus her career on the rights of children. Hillary also worked for the Children's Defense Fund after law school.

Then she moved to Washington, DC. It was 1973. The US Senate was deciding if President Richard Nixon had broken serious campaign laws.

Richard Nixon

Hillary was chosen to help with the investigation. (President Nixon was never put on trial—instead, he resigned on August 9, 1974, the only time in American history that this has happened.)

While Hillary was working in the nation's capital, Bill Clinton was teaching at the University of Arkansas School of Law. Bill was from Arkansas, and he had always planned to return. But he

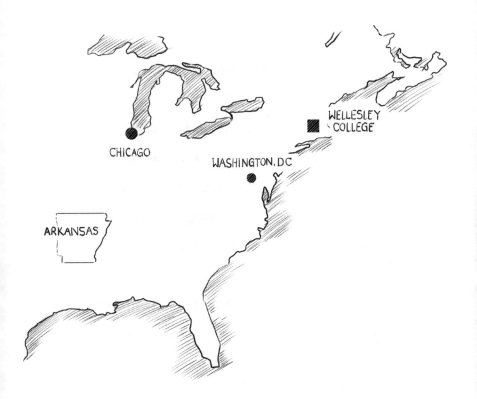

missed Hillary a lot. He asked her to join him.

Move to Arkansas? Her friends thought she was crazy. Hillary had just begun an exciting law career in Washington. Why would she leave for quiet, rural Arkansas?

But Hillary was deeply in love with Bill. In 1974, she followed her heart to Arkansas.

Equal Rights Amendment

Even though women gained the right to vote in 1920, the Constitution (the set of laws people in the United States live by) did not say anything outright about women deserving the same rights as men. Three years later, the Equal Rights Amendment (ERA) was put before Congress. An amendment is something that gets added to the Constitution. For instance, after the Civil War, there was an amendment that made slavery against the law.

The ERA was to guarantee equal rights for women. But the Great Depression, World War II, and the civil rights movement of the 1960s turned the nation's attention away from the women's right movement. Then in 1966, Betty Friedan and twenty-seven other women created the National Organization for Women (NOW).

Betty Friedan

Women banded together to try to pass the ERA. And in 1972, Congress did pass it. But to become an amendment, three-quarters of the fifty states (thirty-eight states) had to approve it. Only thirty-five states did.

To this day, the Equal Rights Amendment is still not in the Constitution.

CHAPTER 4
First Lady of Arkansas

Hillary Rodham and Bill Clinton got married on October 11, 1975.

Before that time, married women usually took their husband's last name. This custom started centuries ago when women were thought to "belong" to their husbands. Hillary decided not to change her name. She would stay Hillary Rodham. Why? Her name was part of who she was. Her identity.

Hillary and Bill bought a house in Fayetteville, Arkansas. Fayetteville is a city in the Ozark Mountains.

In Arkansas, Hillary made many close friends, whom she would keep her whole life. Her friends say that Hillary is extremely loyal and loving. She always remembers everyone's birthdays—even people she doesn't know very well. Best of all, she has a great sense of humor and a *very* loud laugh.

Like Bill, Hillary became a professor at the law school. Students reported that she was a much tougher teacher and grader than Bill.

Bill did not intend to remain a law professor forever. He wanted to be in politics—he wanted to be making laws, not just teaching about them. He ran for attorney general of Arkansas and won. So Bill and Hillary moved to the state capital of Little Rock. In 1978, Bill was elected governor of Arkansas, the youngest governor in the United States.

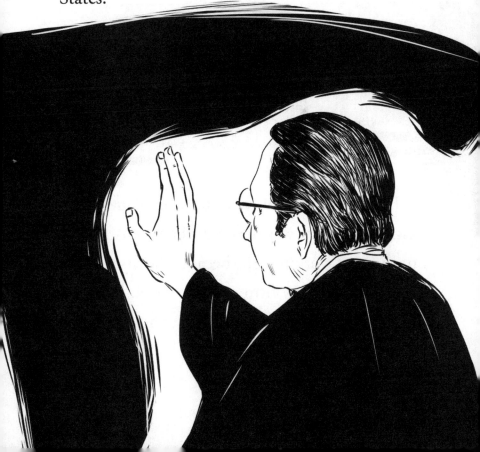

The Clintons moved to the Governor's Mansion. Hillary was now First Lady of Arkansas but she kept working. She became the first female partner at a big law firm in Little Rock. She now earned a lot more money than her husband, the governor!

On February 27, 1980, Hillary gave birth to their daughter, Chelsea Victoria. (Chelsea was named after a popular song called "Chelsea Morning.") At night, Hillary would walk baby Chelsea through the halls of the Governor's Mansion and sing her to sleep—even though Hillary (and her family) admits she has the worst singing voice ever.

Some people thought Hillary should spend more time being the wife of the governor and the mother of a newborn baby. Hillary, however, didn't pay them any mind. She could be a good lawyer, a good mother, *and* a good wife. Then in 1980, Bill ran for governor again and lost. Some people in Arkansas blamed Hillary. They said that she was too strong and outspoken. They said she wasn't pretty. They didn't like the way she dressed. And they didn't like her still using her own name.

Hillary was hurt. She also thought the comments were very unfair. No one would talk about a man's looks or outspoken personality. However, Bill was running for governor again in two years. Hillary didn't want to be the reason that Bill might lose the race.

So she agreed to a makeover. She dyed her hair blonde. She traded in her thick glasses for contact lenses. She began wearing makeup and more fashionable clothes. And she switched her name to Hillary Rodham Clinton.

Making these changes was hard. Hillary always believed that who she was inside mattered more than how she looked. But she wanted to help Bill. She told one of her best friends, "I gave up my name. I got contact lenses. But I'm not going to pretend to be somebody I'm not."

In 1982, Bill Clinton was once again elected Arkansas governor.

The state was among the poorest in the nation. Compared to other states, very few people in Arkansas finished college. Bill put Hillary in charge of a group to fix the school system. Was it because she was his wife? No. Bill gave her the job because he thought she was the best and smartest person for it.

Hillary traveled all over the state to talk with teachers and parents. She made big changes. For example, now all teachers had to take a test to prove their ability to do a good job.

Bill was elected governor again in 1984 and 1986 and 1990. During this time, Hillary worked as a lawyer, hosted events as governor's wife, and helped bring better schools to the state.

Still, she always found time to sit in the bleachers with the other parents and watch Chelsea's softball games. The people of Arkansas grew to appreciate Hillary.

As for Bill, his eyes were turning toward Washington, DC, the capital of the country. His dream was to become president of the United States.

Bill Clinton

William Jefferson Clinton was born on August 19, 1946, in Hope, Arkansas. He became the forty-second president of the United States in 1992, and served two terms. Bill Clinton was president during one of the longest times of peace and economic growth in American history. But his years in office saw many scandals. In 1998, charges were brought against President Clinton for lying about a romance with a young woman working in the White House. The House of Representatives voted to impeach Clinton, to remove him as president. But the Senate didn't agree. Bill Clinton remained president.

Today, Bill Clinton writes books and gives speeches. He has set up the Clinton Foundation to help solve problems in countries around the world.

CHAPTER 5
The Hillary Problem

George H. W. Bush

In 1992, Bill Clinton ran for President of the United States. He was the Democratic candidate and his opponent was President George H. W. Bush, a Republican who hoped to win a second term.

Hillary campaigned with Bill, encouraging people to vote for her husband. One day in a speech, Bill remarked, "Vote for me and you get two for the price of one." He called this a "twofer."

He meant that the American people would get two leaders instead of one—Hillary and him.

To Bill, this was a great deal. He and Hillary had always worked side by side. He thought America would support this kind of partnership between the president and First Lady.

He was wrong.

The First Lady is not an elected office. The First Lady is the wife of the president. She does not have any political power. So what Bill said made a lot of Americans worry. Would Hillary be running the country with Bill? Would she be a co-president?

Soon, newspapers and TV shows began calling this "the Hillary problem."

The Hillary Problem

Hillary tried to defend herself. But she made it worse by reminding people how she had never just "stayed home and baked cookies."

Many people thought this comment meant Hillary looked down on women who stayed home with their families. But she didn't. She had gone on to say she wanted women to be able to choose what to do with their lives. But on TV, that part of her comment was never played.

Hillary had always been a very private person. But from then on, she was even more guarded when she spoke. "I've learned to be more careful in what I say," she said, "because I really don't mind having people disagree with me so long as they are disagreeing with what I really believe or say."

Hillary never stopped campaigning for Bill. He won the election. And in January of 1993, Hillary, Bill, and Chelsea moved into the White House as America's First Family. They brought

their black-and-white cat named
Socks. On their first day there,
Hillary made a scavenger hunt
for Chelsea and her friends,
so she could learn her way
around the big mansion.

Family life changed a lot. They had Secret
Service agents following them and protecting
them at all times. Hillary was given the code name

of "Evergreen." Bill's was "Eagle," and Chelsea's was "Energy." But Hillary always made sure they had family dinners at the kitchen table. Hillary liked living in the White House—especially having the chef bake her favorite mocha mousse cake as a midnight snack.

Chelsea Clinton

Chelsea was twelve years old when her father was elected president of the United States. She liked exploring the White House—132 rooms in all. But she didn't like when reporters made fun of her. Her parents told the press that Chelsea was "off-limits." They wanted her to have as normal a childhood as possible.

In 1997, Chelsea went to college at Stanford University in California. Even away from the White House, she stayed in the spotlight. Her dorm room was given bulletproof windows. Secret Service agents lived in her building and disguised themselves as students.

After college, Chelsea studied at Oxford University in England. Then she joined NBC as a reporter. In 2014, Chelsea and her husband, Marc Mezvinsky, had a baby girl named Charlotte. A baby boy named Aidan followed in 2016. Today, Chelsea works for the Clinton Foundation. Like her mother, she speaks out for women's rights and human rights around the world.

CHAPTER 6
FLOTUS

Before moving into the White House, Hillary decided to give up her job as a partner in a law firm.

The question was, what would she do now as First Lady of the United States (or FLOTUS)? She wanted to play a part in government. So Hillary read about all the First Ladies before her. She admired Eleanor Roosevelt the most. Eleanor was involved with many causes. She wrote a newspaper column and spoke out for human rights. Hillary decided to be like that, too.

Bill wanted Hillary to work on changing health care so that poor people in the United States could count on seeing good doctors without paying a lot of money. Other countries, such as Great Britain, did this. So why not the United States?

Helping to change medical care was exactly the kind of work that meant the most to Hillary. She took an office in the West Wing of the White House. (That's where the president and his aides work. Before this, First Ladies always stayed in offices in the East Wing.)

WEST WING   EAST WING

Eleanor Roosevelt (1884–1962)

Eleanor Roosevelt was First Lady for twelve years (1933–1945). During the first term of her husband, Franklin Delano Roosevelt, many banks and businesses closed down. People lost their jobs.

They were hungry. This terrible time was called the Great Depression. A victim of polio, Franklin D. Roosevelt could not walk, so Eleanor took his place, traveling all around the country, bringing hope to people. She gave speeches about women's rights, children's rights, and the rights of the homeless. She gave the money she earned from the speeches to the poor.

When the United States entered World War II in 1941, Eleanor went to work for the Red Cross. She visited wounded American soldiers all over Asia and Europe. When the war ended, she became the United States' representative at the new United Nations. After her death in 1962, *Time* magazine called her the "world's most admired and talked about woman."

Hillary was put in charge of coming up with a health care plan and convincing Congress to vote for it.

It didn't happen.

Hillary worked hard, but many people thought the plan was too complicated. Still, Hillary tried to push the plan forward, often stubbornly refusing to listen to other ideas. People complained that she was difficult and demanding. Hillary failed to get the support of powerful politicians. In 1994, the president's team dropped the plan.

Hillary was stunned. She had never failed at something so big or so publicly. "I learned some valuable lessons about . . . taking small steps to get a big job done," Hillary later admitted.

The defeat was hard, but Hillary did not fade into the background. She turned to other issues. Hillary spoke out for the rights of children and women. She began a program that made the states pay for health care for children whose parents didn't have enough money to pay for doctors. She was also responsible for a law that made it easier for parents to adopt children.

Hillary traveled more than any other First Lady—to eighty-two countries! On almost every trip, she talked about women's rights, health care, or child care. In a speech she gave while visiting China, she said, "Human rights are women's rights, and women's rights are human rights."

Hillary wrote her own weekly newspaper column, just as Eleanor Roosevelt had done. She called it "Talking It Over." Hillary also wrote a best-selling book called *It Takes a Village*. The book was about how every child needs a

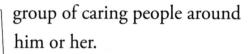

group of caring people around him or her.

Bill Clinton was president for two terms, or eight years. During that time, Hillary learned a lot about politics, how the government and the people in it worked, and how to best handle the news media. She learned what people liked and disliked about her, too.

All these lessons would come in handy in the future.

CHAPTER 7
Into the Spotlight

In 2000, Bill Clinton's presidency was almost over, and Chelsea was away at college. Hillary had to decide what to do next in her life. She had spent years helping Bill get elected and govern. Now Hillary had political dreams of her own, and it was time for her to chase them. She decided to run for the US Senate. The Senate writes and votes on new laws. The Senate has one hundred members—two from each state.

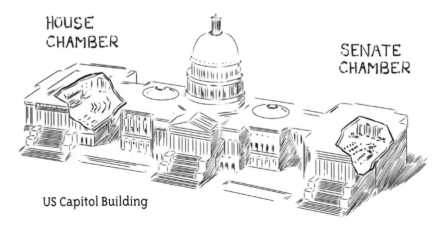

HOUSE CHAMBER

SENATE CHAMBER

US Capitol Building

Although she had lived in Arkansas for many years and had grown up in Illinois, Hillary did not run for senator in either of those states. She chose New York, instead. An older senator from New York was retiring. New York had an opening for a new senator. Maybe New Yorkers would welcome a female Democratic candidate.

Hillary and Bill moved to Chappaqua, New York, a town about forty miles from New York City. (She had to live in New York State before she could run for senator from the state.)

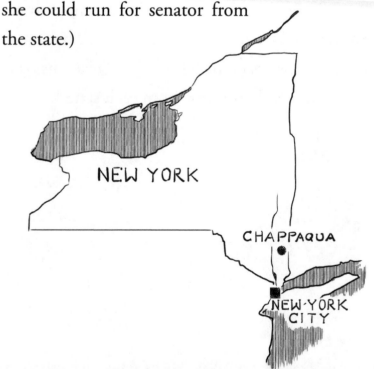

NEW YORK

CHAPPAQUA

NEW YORK CITY

After a year, she began to campaign. The man she was running against called her a "pushy woman." Hillary had heard this many times before! Would his comment hurt her? Not this time. New Yorkers liked her intelligence and her strength. They elected her to the Senate in 2000. Hillary was no longer a politician's wife. Now *she* was the elected politician.

The Clintons' home in Chappaqua

Hillary was the first First Lady to hold an elected office. She was also the first woman to be elected senator from New York.

The very first year she was in office, something terrible happened. The deadliest attack ever in the United States took place. On September 11, 2001, terrorists flew two airplanes into the Twin Towers in New York City and killed almost three thousand innocent people.

A third plane hit the Pentagon building outside Washington, DC, killing 184 people. (The Pentagon is the US military headquarters.) A fourth plane, believed to also be heading to Washington, DC, crashed in Pennsylvania.

The whole country was in shock.

Lower Manhattan was ground zero—the center—of the attack. Buildings were destroyed. Dust and debris lay everywhere. As the new senator from New York, Hillary worked hard to help Lower Manhattan recover. She made sure the government paid billions of dollars for the cleanup and to treat the health problems of people who helped with the cleanup effort.

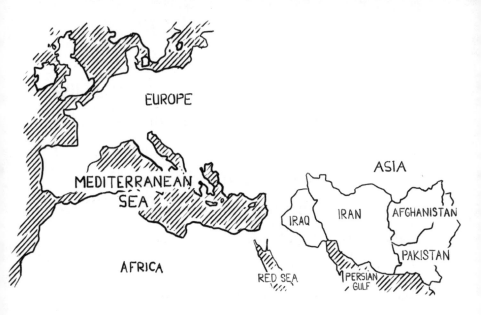

EUROPE

MEDITERRANEAN SEA

ASIA

IRAQ   IRAN   AFGHANISTAN

AFRICA

RED SEA   PERSIAN GULF

PAKISTAN

After the terrorist attack, the United States declared war on the country of Afghanistan. That was where Osama bin Laden, the terrorists' leader, had lived and worked. Later on, President George W. Bush believed that the country of Iraq was helping the terrorists and making powerful weapons that could destroy thousands of people. So he pushed to go to war there, too. He needed the vote of the Senate, which agreed (77–23) to attack Iraq. Hillary was among the senators who backed the president.

As the war dragged on for many years, however, Hillary began to speak against it. She didn't like having US troops over there for so long. She didn't like that President Bush was spending billions of dollars on the war but cutting back on education and programs that helped the poor in the United States. Worst of all, the terrible weapons did not even exist. The United States had gone into a deadly and costly war for false reasons.

Hillary's "yes" vote for the war haunted her. "I made a mistake, plain and simple," she admitted more than ten years later.

Nevertheless, the people of New York liked having Hillary as their senator. They reelected her in 2006. She got 67 percent of the votes! All along, though, New Yorkers guessed that Hillary had her sights set on a higher office.

They were right.

A presidential election was coming up in November of 2008. In 2007, Hillary Clinton made a big announcement. She wanted to run as the Democratic candidate. And she planned to win.

HILLARYCLINTON.COM
Hillary *for President*

Political Parties

What is a political party? It is a group of voters with many of the same views about how the government should work. In the United States, there are two main political parties—Democratic and Republican.

The Democratic Party was started in 1792. Democrats believe that the government should help make people's lives better. For instance, the government should play a big role in providing education, health care, and jobs.

The Democratic Party symbol is the donkey.

The Republican Party was started in 1854. Over time, Republicans came to believe that the government should play a smaller role in people's lives. The Republican Party symbol is the elephant.

Their nickname is the GOP, which stands for Grand Old Party.

There are many other smaller political parties, too, such as the Green Party and the Libertarian Party.

If you don't want to be a part of a party, you are called an independent voter.

CHAPTER 8
Making History

Hillary couldn't just decide on her own to be the Democratic candidate for president. Elections for president don't work that way. She had to be chosen by her party in early elections—called primaries—that many states hold.

In a state primary election, Democrats run only against other Democrats, and Republicans run only against other Republicans. After the presidential primaries are over, the Democratic candidate and the Republican candidate face off in a general election. (That election is held every four years, on a Tuesday in early November.)

"I am in to win!" Hillary said about becoming the Democratic candidate for president. And, indeed, she was expected to win. After all, she was a household name—a woman known to everyone in the country. She had been First Lady, and now she was a popular senator from a powerful state.

Hillary traveled all over the country meeting voters and debating other Democratic candidates. At first, it looked as if Hillary could beat them all. A lot of people felt Hillary acted as if the nomination was a sure thing. However, in politics, nothing is a sure thing.

A Democratic senator from Illinois was getting a lot of attention. His name was Barack Obama. He was young and smart and devoted to the same causes as Hillary.

Barack Obama

Like Hillary, Barack Obama was also trying to make history. He wanted to be the first African American elected as president.

The primary races between Hillary and Barack Obama were close. In total, more than seventeen and a half million people voted for Hillary. But in the end, more voted for Barack Obama, and he became the Democratic candidate for president.

Losing wasn't easy for Hillary. She was upset and frustrated. She had tried to show America that she would make a stronger and better president. She wasn't sure people had seen her witty and caring side. But she knew that her campaign had changed the way many Americans viewed women in politics. The question no longer was: *Can* a woman be president? The question had changed to: *When* will a woman be president?

In a speech, Hillary said, "I was proud to be running as a woman, but I was running because I thought I'd be the best president. But I am a woman, and like millions of women, I know there are still barriers and biases out there . . . I want to build an America that respects and embraces the potential of every last one of us."

Even though they had been rivals, Barack Obama wanted, and needed, Hillary's support to win the election in November. She agreed. In fact, she promised to give an important speech for him at the Democratic National Convention. (The convention is where the party's candidate is announced.)

Women Who Ran for President

No woman has yet been elected as president of the United States. But that doesn't mean that women haven't tried. In fact, more than thirty-five women have run.

Victoria Woodhull was the first woman to run for president. In 1872, she ran as part of the Equal Rights Party. She was

Victoria Woodhull

an early feminist and suffragette. Her campaign was mostly symbolic, which meant she was trying to prove a point more than trying to win.

In 1884 and 1888, attorney Belva Ann Lockwood ran as a candidate from the National Equal Rights Party.

Belva Lockwood

Belva was the first woman to argue a case before the Supreme Court, the highest US court.

Fast forward eighty years . . . In 1964, Margaret Chase Smith, a senator from Maine, tried to become the

Margaret Chase Smith

Republican presidential candidate.

Then in 1972, Democratic congresswoman Shirley Chisholm became the first African American woman to run for president.

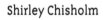

Shirley Chisholm

Hillary had always taught Chelsea to "be gracious in defeat." Now Hillary showed that. Hillary encouraged all Americans to vote for Barack Obama. They were not rivals anymore.

CHAPTER 9
Madam Secretary

Barack Obama won the presidential election on November 4, 2008. Five days later, President Obama called Hillary. He wanted her to be his secretary of state. He told one of his top aides he chose Hillary because "she's smart; she's tough; she has status in the world."

Secretary of state is one of the most powerful jobs in the US government. The secretary of state advises the president on problems around the world. She also meets with the heads of other countries to work out disagreements. A good secretary of state helps to keep the United States and the world at peace.

At first, Hillary decided not to take the job. Why? She felt she owed it to the people of New York to finish out her term as their elected senator. (A Senate term is six years, so Hillary still had four years to go.)

But every time she called the new president, he refused to get on the phone. He didn't want to hear her say no. Finally, he picked up. He told her that America needed her. She was good at bringing people together, and she knew so much about foreign issues.

The next morning Hillary accepted. "When your president asks you to serve, you should say

yes," she said. Hillary became the third woman and the only former First Lady to be secretary of state. She served from 2009 to 2013.

Being secretary of state was very demanding. But Hillary had amazing energy. She traveled to 112 countries, flying almost a million miles! She traveled to more countries than any other secretary of state had before. Hillary believed it was important to meet world leaders face-to-face.

When countries in the Middle East had uprisings, she urged them to set up democratic governments. She helped gather aid when there were natural disasters, such as the earthquakes in Haiti and Chile and the floods in Pakistan. And she continued to fight for women's and children's rights around the world. Hillary called fighting for women's rights "the cause of my life."

Hillary in 2011 standing with Meera Shankar,
Ambassasor from India

Being secretary of state had what some called the "Hillary effect." It showed other nations what a smart, powerful woman could accomplish. By the end of 2009, twenty-five countries had sent female ambassadors to Washington. (Ambassadors are government officials who represent their countries abroad.) This was the highest number of women ever.

In February 2013, Hillary resigned as secretary of state. President Obama said, "I think Hillary will go down as one of the finest secretaries of state we've had."

After leaving office, Hillary finally took time to relax. She swam. She did yoga. She took long walks with Bill and their dogs. She read *Goodnight Moon* to her new granddaughter, who was born on September 26, 2014.

But Hillary wasn't good at relaxing. She liked to be busy. So she published a book called *Hard Choices,* about her time as secretary of state. She traveled throughout the country giving hundreds of speeches.

And everywhere she went, everyone asked her the same question: Will you run again for president?

Hillary never gave an answer . . . until April 2015.

Leaders of Their Country

Golda Meir (1898–1978) was one of the founders and leaders of Israel, which became a country in 1948. In 1969, at age seventy, she became the first woman to be prime minister (the head of the country).

Golda Meir

Indira Gandhi (1917–1984) was the daughter of Jawaharlal Nehru, the first prime minister of India, which claimed its independence from Great Britain in 1947. In 1966, she became India's first female prime minister.

Indira Gandhi

Margaret Thatcher (1925–2013) was the first female prime minister of the United Kingdom. She was elected in 1979 and served three terms. In 2016, Theresa May became the second woman to hold Great Britain's highest office.

Margaret Thatcher

Angela Merkel (1954–) is the first female chancellor (head of the government) of Germany. First elected in 2005, she won a fourth term in 2017, making her the longest-serving elected head of state in Europe.

Angela Merkel

CHAPTER 10
The 2016 Election

In April 2015, Hillary Rodham Clinton announced that she would try again to become the first woman president of the United States. The election would be on November 8, 2016.

NOVEMBER 2016

SUNDAY	MONDAY	TUESDAY	WEDNESDAY	THURSDAY	FRIDAY	SATURDAY
		1	2	3	4	5
6	7	8	9	10	11	12
13	14	15	16	17	18	19

Hillary announced her new campaign in a video that showed ordinary families preparing for big days in their lives. "Everyday Americans need a champion, and I want to be that champion," Hillary said.

Hillary said that this campaign would be very different from her last campaign. In 2008, she believed being a female candidate would hurt her. She thought people would not see her as tough enough. So she didn't make a big deal about being the first woman president. And she rarely spoke about the women's and family issues that had always been so important to her.

Times changed. Hillary hired many more women for her campaign. Hillary talked a lot about women's issues, such as childcare, paid family leave, and equal pay. She pointed out that these weren't only women's issues—they affected all Americans. "We know that when women are strong, families are strong," Hillary said. "When families are strong, countries are strong."

This time around, Hillary focused more on the American people and less on proving herself. She brought even more skill, knowledge, and experience to this campaign. She had been First Lady, a US senator, and secretary of state.

Although Hillary was so well known, she wanted to reintroduce herself to voters. After announcing her new campaign, Hillary jumped into a van and rode more than one thousand

miles from her home in New York to rural Iowa, stopping along the way to talk to small groups. She hoped people would have the chance to really get to know Hillary Rodham Clinton—the passionate activist, the hardworking woman, the loving grandmother, and the feminist.

Hillary had a tough primary battle. Her main opponent was Bernie Sanders, a longtime independent senator from Vermont. Younger voters really liked him. Why? One reason was his pledge to make the government, not students,

Bernie Sanders

pay for the cost of college. His campaign received more small, individual donations (3.25 million!) than any other candidate. The average donation was just $27.00. Sanders was a popular candidate, but was he able to stop Hillary? No!

On June 6, 2016, Hillary was declared the Democratic Party's candidate for president. The first woman ever!

Now it was on to the general election. Who would Hillary run against? The Republican Party's candidate was a big surprise.

Donald J. Trump was a well-known billionaire

businessman who owned many hotels and other real estate. He was also a reality-TV star. But he had never held an elected office. He promised voters to lower taxes and make better trade deals for America with other countries. He also wanted to build a wall between Mexico and the United States to keep people from crossing into the country illegally.

Hillary wanted to raise taxes for the richest people in America, and she was opposed to Trump's ideas on immigration. Instead, she promised to help immigrants become citizens. She also stood for stricter laws on who could own guns, and she supported prison reform.

Hillary and Donald had three debates in front of huge television and streaming audiences. The first debate was watched by more than 84 million viewers! The debates highlighted the bitter tone of the campaign. Many people thought it was the nastiest campaign they'd ever seen.

Voters questioned the moral character of both candidates. Many didn't like how Donald acted toward minorities and women. But many doubted Hillary's judgment and trustworthiness. As secretary of state, she had sent work emails through a private, unsecured network. She was not supposed to do that.

Finally, voters went to the polls and made their choice. More than sixty-five million Americans voted for Hillary—almost three million more votes than Donald Trump received. Hillary had won the popular vote. But Donald won more electoral votes, so he was the winner. On January 20, 2017, Donald J. Trump became the forty-fifth president of the United States.

The morning after the election, Hillary spoke to her supporters in New York City. "This loss hurts," she said, "but please never stop believing that fighting for what's right is worth it." It was everyone's responsibility, she said, to build a "better, stronger, fairer America."

"And to all the little girls who are watching this," Hillary continued, "never doubt that you are valuable and powerful and deserving of every chance and opportunity . . . to pursue and achieve your own dreams. . . . If we stand together . . . our best days are still ahead of us."

Timeline of
Hillary Clinton's Life

1947	Hillary Diane Rodham is born on October 26
1961	Attends Maine East High School in Park Ridge, Illinois
1962	Goes with church youth group to hear Reverend Martin Luther King Jr. in Chicago
1965	Enrolls at Wellesley College in Wellesley, Massachusetts
1969	Graduates Wellesley with a degree in political science
	Begins Yale Law School in New Haven, Connecticut
1970	Works for civil rights lawyer Marian Wright Edelman
1973	Begins work as an attorney for the Children's Defense Fund
1974	Moves to Arkansas
1975	Marries Bill Clinton on October 11
1979	Named full partner at Rose Law Firm
1980	Chelsea Victoria Clinton is born on February 27
1993	Becomes First Lady of the United States
	Leads the Task Force on National Health Care Reform
2000	Elected to the US Senate from New York
2008	Loses Democratic nomination for president to Illinois Senator Barack Obama
2009	Becomes US secretary of state
2015	Announces that she will run for US president in 2016
2016	On June 6, becomes the first woman nominated by a major political party to run for US president
	On November 8, loses general election to Donald J. Trump

Timeline of the World

1945	World War II ends
1954	The Vietnam War begins
1963	Martin Luther King Jr. gives his "I Have a Dream" speech
1966	Indira Gandhi becomes the first woman prime minister of India
1969	Golda Meir becomes the first woman prime minister of Israel
1974	President Richard Nixon resigns
1979	Margaret Thatcher becomes the first woman prime minister of Great Britain
1981	Sandra Day O'Connor becomes the first woman appointed to the US Supreme Court
1984	Geraldine Ferraro is the first woman nominated for vice president of the United States
1992	Bill Clinton is elected President of the United States
1997	Madeleine Albright is the first woman US secretary of state
2001	On September 11, terrorists attack the World Trade Center in New York City and the Pentagon near Washington, DC
2003	Iraq War begins
2005	Angela Merkel elected chancellor of Germany
2009	Barack Obama becomes the first African American president of the United States
2017	Donald J. Trump becomes the forty-fifth US president

Bibliography

* Books for young readers

Allen, Jonathan, and Amie Parnes. *HRC: State Secrets and the Rebirth of Hillary Clinton*. New York: Crown Publishers, 2014.

*Doak, Robin S. *Hillary Clinton*. New York: Scholastic, 2013.

*Guernsey, JoAnn Bren. *Hillary Rodham Clinton*. Minneapolis: Twenty-First Century Books, 2010.

*Krull, Kathleen. *Hillary Rodham Clinton: Dreams Taking Flight*. New York: Simon & Schuster, 2008.

*Lee, Sally. *Hillary Clinton*. Minnesota: Capstone Press, 2011.

Rodham Clinton, Hillary. *Hard Choices*. New York: Simon & Schuster, 2014.

Rodham Clinton, Hillary. *Living History*. New York: Simon & Schuster, 2003.

Sheehy, Gail. *Hillary's Choice*. New York: Random House, 1999.